ink & air

short poems for faraway friends

megs thompson

foreword by ingrid h. turner

ink & air

short poems for faraway friends

is a work of my own creation.

ISBN - 978-1-961185-38-8

Cover, Book Design, and Layout by megs thompson
megswrites llc - www.megswrites.com

www.inomniaparatuspublishing.com

this collection is for you,
my fellow human, doing the best you
can each & every day.

remember to slow down,
smell the rain,
feed the squirrels,
bask in the sun,
dance in the kitchen,
hug those you love
& cry, as often as necessary.

foreword

Poetry is vulnerable.

Really vulnerable.

I think that's why so many new poets hide behind big words and lofty ideas. They have the gift – no doubt – of touching the underbelly of life, but it's still too tender to expose to an audience, to dance with it in the open.

It's a great poet who brings the depth of existence to us on everyday language, in casual vignettes, wrenching open the substance of life through little words and relatable sonnets. That's what Megs does here, in her debut collection of poetry. She is by no means a novice, clearly, with over three hundred pieces of writing in her first go!

Megs does something with her writing that only those who have faced themselves head on can do. She reaches down and grabs hold of the essence of the human experience and brings to life the wordless and the universal through beautiful simplicity.

Reading Megs' words is like talking to an old friend with many shared memories – so much of the conversation is underneath the language. Somehow, Megs does that for strangers on paper, with her poetry.

Ingrid H. Turner
Poet & Mystic

dear reader,

the humble collection you're currently holding was once nothing more than a crazy idea to write a single short poem every day for a full year, affix my words to the back of a postcard & send them into the wind, bound for a stranger somewhere in the world.

what i didn't realize was that over the course of that single year, those poems, the brief moments of quiet reflection when i allowed myself to bask in the world around me, the mundane, the ordinary, they would change my life forever.

over the course of that year i lost friends, i found myself & i fell in love. i went on adventures, physically, emotionally & spiritually. i learned lessons, i made mistakes, i laughed & i cried.

and now, i've taken those 365 poems, previously seen only by the strangers who received them via post & combined them here, into my own ramshackle collection of ink & air.

megs thompson
may 2024

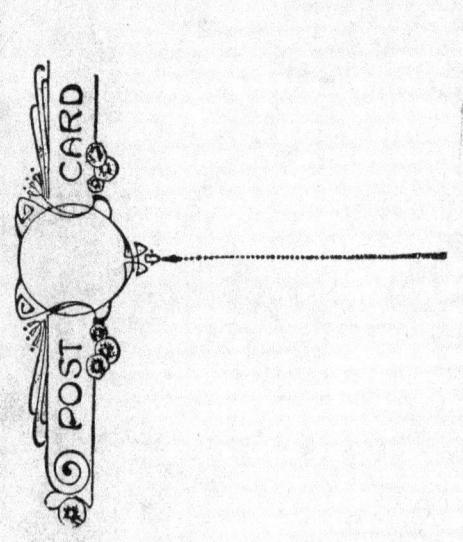

POST CARD

1 gulls
congregate
at the waters'
edge
just beyond
reach
of the rolling
waves
contemplating
how to fill
the day
ahead

2 the quaint
british family
the childrens'
lilted speech
hinting
at possession
homicidal
tendencies
trying
tirelessly
to capture
the attention
of mummy

3 they mingle
the conversations
forced
unnatural
uncomfortable
mortgage payments
divorce settlements
career achievements
every breath
bragging
pushing
their status
a notch above
the others
in audience
reminiscing
on their youth

4 winding through
the forest
it's easy
to forget
the world
outside
the shelter
of trees

5   she mumbles
     softly
     aching
     to not disturb
     the conversations
     surrounding her
     she confesses
     to a stranger
     her desire
     to be free
     to love
     to marry
     to live
     with the woman
     of her dreams

6   he stands
     back pressed
     against the wall
     trying
     his best
     to sink
     into the decades old
     structure
     to be anywhere
     but here

7   an early morning
     stroll
     weaving between giants
     big cedars
     natures' barcode
     towering
     over a silent
     winding
     creek
     suckling
     at the teat
     of its ocean mother

8   i watch
     hiding my smile
     with the pages
     of the book
     in which i feign
     interest
     as she helps
     her father
     a man of no less
     than 80
     climb atop
     a high chair
     barstool
     for a pint
     of well pulled stout

9 fuzzy bees
  buzzing
  bumbling
  bloomers
  formed from
  pilfered pollen
  humming
  as they work

10 the barn
  stands
  hardly
  a skeletal
  reminder
  of a time
  way of life
  country
  long passed

11 a single face
  peers at us
  from within
  the safety
  of a haphazardly
  constructed
  nest
  it's eyes
  blinking
  shocked
  beneath premature
  feather tufts
  an aviary
  monks tonsure
  overwhelmed
  yet not shying
  away
  from the world

12 the baby sparrow
  is sending signs
  on the sun
  scorched wind
  that he likes me
  too

I3 it's comical
    the ways in which
    a woman's face
    contorts
    twists
    stretches
    as if demon
    possessed
    a never ending
    quest
    to paint
    every
    curve
    of her lip

I4 how is it
    time flashes
    as i fall
    into a mountainous
    thicket
    the thorns
    of mother nature's
    most intrusively
    delicious
    gatekeeper
    all for the plucking
    of the biggest
    juiciest
    most seductive
    berry

I5 he holds a hastily
    scrawled sign
    a proclamation
    of his truth
    this is what
    invisible looks like
    as the city
    continues
    unfaltering
    passing him by

I6 he was strong
    a man of
    independence
    pride
    unshakable morals
    an open heart
    belly laughs
    wide grins
    sparkling eyes
    magic

17 how is it
time stands
still
as i balance
precariously
atop this weather worn
wooden chair
questioning
my
life choices
maturity
decision making
skills
knowing
that at any
moment
the clock will
start again
mother nature
will chuckle
and i will
fall

18 my grandmother still
lives here
within my childhood
home
her home too
before her brain
told her
to end it all
she walks through the
rooms
shuffling the pages
of my books
casting a shadow
along the wall
leaning ever so
softly
against the kitchen
door jamb
her presence smudging
the decades-old
markers
of my youth

19 they tell me i look
   like her
   in the face
   that i've inherited
   her deep laugh
   her rosy apple
   cheeks
   her dimples & her
   height
   a woman i know only
   through pilfered
   photographs
   long past their
   prime
   now yellowed
   with age
   a woman of strong
   will
   independence & pride
   the woman who raised
   my father

20 he tells me
   this man
   with sparkling blue
   eyes
   fingers stained
   nicotine gold
   and more than one
   empty glass
   before him at the bar
   god decided
   to pack up his
   knapsack
   and head for
   somewhere
   new
   leaving mary & jesus
   to run the show
   he's grown tired
   of hearing
   the never ending
   monotonous
   whines
   echoing from here
   below

21 they met
when he returned from
'nam
he was hitchhiking
headed anywhere
else
she rescued
him
offered a ride
unlocking
the passenger side
inviting him to join
her
on the cracked
vinyl bench seat
until death
do them part

22 he's been my
companion
my four legged
protector
confidante
sounding board
therapist
cuddle buddy
friend
keeping me safe
mentally
physically
emotionally
until he knew
there was someone
you
worthy
of taking his place

23 they met
on an overnight
business flight
nashville to wichita
she brought him
peanuts
checked his safety
belt
watched
for his luggage
on the deserted
turnstile
the airport
empty
echoing with the
souls
of travelers
long departed
she followed him
home
and hasn't left
since

24 i keep waking up
and losing
who i am
he confesses
panic shaking
the breath
behind
his words

25 he remembers me
in spurts
flashes
of who he was
before
he calls me
devilish
with a flirty
grin
bringing tears
memories
of the man
he used to be

26 he questions
who he is
why
he's still
here
imprisoned within a
body
fighting
against him
a mind
intent on deceit
the tremors
having long ago
overtaken
his hands
will
faith
that things will
improve
that tomorrow
will be better
that the sun
will rise again

27 how is it
they know
without a single
word
interaction
that i'm an empath
sensitive
to their every fear
frustration
angst
confusion
regret
desire

28 how is it
they know
that i'll listen
without
judgment
interruption
that i'll remain
here
seemingly unshakable
as they purge
their conscience
to a stranger
naturally attuned
to hear them out

29 she berates
   my boyfriend
   the man who serves
   as my sensitive
   reasonable
   even keeled
   level
   she's unstable
   aggressive
   she thinks
   i'm lying
   when i sit here
   before her
   a silent observer
   of her anger
   at the world

30 she yells
   about racism
   rape
   school shootings
   ruth bader ginsburg
   the clinton
   administration
   toxic
   masculinity
   sex trafficking
   her voice
   cracks
   deep
   coated with years
   of pall mall
   fear
   hate
   dissatisfaction
   with life

3I autumn brings
   crisp mornings
   reverting back
   to hot coffee
   mulled spiced cider
   naked trees
   spreading puddles
   calm

32 the drum beat
   replaces
   that of my own
   heart
   the crowd
   a mass
   of strangers
   shedding
   their culturally
   approved
   inhibitions
   their rocking
   bodies
   forming one
   primal
   beast

33 autumn brings
   a uniform
   of comfort
   sweaters
   socks
   shoes
   with laces
   a contrast
   to the naked
   reckless
   abandon
   of summer

34 he releases them
   the coils
   tendrils
   erupting
   from within
   his skull
   once tamed
   harnessed
   now thrashing
   attacking
   all
   within their reach
   this modern day
   punk rock
   medusa

35 a broken heart
   st nds
   the other piece
   with a friend
   seemingly
   from another life
   another time
   lost
   decades ago

36 wooden beads
   plastic barrettes
   tarnished chains
   a crisp 2 dollar bill
   punk haired trolls
   tiny dinosaurs
   a gold cross pendant
   my first
   string of pearls
   a childhood jewelry
   box
   filled
   with items
   priceless
   memories
   of innocence

37 i watched
   in horror
   my body
   locked in place
   refusing
   to obey
   the screams
   emanating
   from within
   my heart
   mind

38 he trembled
   convulsed
   fought
   against the
   restraints
   biting
   into the paper
   thin skin
   of his wrists

39 his eyes
   lock with mine
   a shared
   unspoken
   conversation
   a moment
   of clarity
   amidst the confusion
   dementia
   a moment
   when he was
   back

40 his voice
   no more than a
   whisper
   a ghost
   of his past
   some would have
   called it
   violence
   abuse
   neglect
   insanity
   in our house
   it was love
   it was normal
   it was mom

4I we are not
   accidents
   the sign reads
   etched in chalk
   the board
   no longer black
   foggy
   with the dust
   remnants
   of wisdom
   long since erased

42 i am
   a beautiful
   contradiction
   simply
   complicated
   sensitively
   strong

43 will i forget
   the color
   of my mother's hair
   silver
   like the tinsel
   so dreaded
   in my youth

   will i forget
   the pitch of her
   laugh
   full bodied
   resounding
   from the depths
   of her spirit

44 they sit
   together
   alone
   immersed
   in their personal
   devices
   holding
   their attention
   instead of
   holding hands
   keeping them
   from connecting
   to anything
   everything
   but high speed
   wifi

45 i lie here
   vulnerable
   like never before
   my heart
   naked
   unguarded
   against your love
   adoration

46 the bruises
   scars
   evidence
   of battles
   fought
   won
   so often hidden
   beneath
   makeup
   long sleeves
   thick skin
   guarded heart

17 it was a different
time
we
as a country
as a people
fought
for basic rights
focused
on equality
for all
not just those
that sparkle
and scream
the loudest

it was a different
time
we
as a country
as a people
sacrificed
gave life
no expectation
no reward
for greater good
believed
in the good
of our fellow
man

it was a different
time
we
as a country
as a people
held ourselves
each other
to a higher
standard

48 he stands
   on the sidelines
   watching
   dictating
   a maestro
   directing
   never assisting
   for fear of breaking
   the unspoken
   line
   that separates
   him
   from
   the help

49 the pomp
   ceremony
   hypnotic chanting
   swinging incense
   a chorus of voices
   resonate
   echo
   between the pillars

50 his voice
   gets louder
   carries
   across
   the crowded
   space
   with every
   drink
   he imbibes
   his opinions
   grow
   stronger
   his sensibilities
   grow
   thinner

5I he beats her
   resorting to
   words
   when distance
   prevents
   his fist from
   landing home

52 they speak
   to quell the silence
   to distract
   from the resounding
   universal voice
   of reason
   right
   wrong

   they speak
   to deploy a stream
   of sentences
   syllables
   to fill the void
   with mutterings
   ramblings
   of a madman

   they speak
   in fear of being left
   with the glaring
   clarity
   truth
   vulnerability
   of ones own
   thoughts

53 we're trespassing
   slipping past
   statues of saints
   frozen
   in time
   the virgin
   mother
   cradling
   their savior

54 they've argued
   for always
   their words
   voices
   echoing
   throughout
   the memories
   of my youth

55 the moon
   barely a sliver
   a white
   crescent
   tip
   of gods
   thumbnail
   as he watches
   quietly
   from above

56 i held you
   as your lungs
   released
   one last breath
   of life
   the poison
   beckoning you
   away
   from the pain
   confusion
   frustration
   stealing you
   away
   from me

57 i held you
as your heart
beat
it's last
you've been
my companion
protector
confidante
in a world
where being
quiet
is seen as being
weak
you were my
voice

i held you
as you relaxed
the muscles
of your suddenly
small form
your head resting
nestled snuggly
in the curve
of my neck
collar bone
i slowed my breath
to mirror yours
deliberate
soft
i held you
tighter
breathing
you in

POST CARD

United States
& Canada
One Cent.

Foreign
Two Cents.

For Address Only.

For Correspondence.

"Snowflake" Series-Christmas-Postcard No. 1204. Printed in Vienna.

58 leaves
   shuffle
   frost
   bitten
   lazily
   to the ground

59 droplets of rain
   halted
   on their way
   down
   to earth
   puddles
   frozen
   on their way
   back
   up

60 a gorgeous
   hypnotic
   curtain
   blurring the world
   dividing here
   from there
   a milky
   translucent screen
   protecting us
   from the sun
   ensuring
   the spookiness
   of fall

6I the mother
   shoots
   wispy
   noodle-like
   starts
   saplings
   across the expanse
   of cement
   no longer
   drab
   institutional
   but decorated
   with meandering vines
   a plethora
   of red leaves
   forming
   proof
   of life

62 his sweater
   stretched
   pulled
   the sleeves
   collar
   in hopes of hiding
   the ink
   decorating
   his form

63 the crisp
   formless
   biting
   wind
   made visible
   by the dancing
   leaves

64 an echo
   of life
   lived
   the shadow
   of a being
   no longer
   composed
   of material
   but scented
   gusts
   perfumed
   air

65 breath
   formed without
   lungs
   rustling
   the curtain
   teasing
   the flame
   prickling
   the skin
   at the nape
   of my neck

66 i watch
   voyeuristically
   as she stares
   blankly
   expectantly
   aghast
   at the pump
   an oregonian
   a stranger
   in a strange land
   of self service
   fueling

67 named lillian
   for her mother
   called lily
   by those she loves
   for her purity
   innocence
   the sparkle
   in her eyes
   a mother
   grandmother
   body old
   eternally
   young
   in spirit
   and mind

68 she changes
   her mind
   no longer
   confident
   sure
   of her stance
   the choices
   facing her
   relenting
   relinquishing
   to the will
   of another

69 her smile
   assuring us
   herself
   that she's lived
   loved
   with no regrets

70 seven ladies
   all in a row
   their string
   of small
   humble
   apartments
   brick
   to stave off the
   winter
   chill
   widows
   a family formed
   amongst themselves
   here
   miles detached
   from their
   congregation
   their leader
   messiah

71 they rely
   on one another
   for companionship
   prayer
   guidance
   coffee creamer
   waiting
   patiently
   for the next
   prophecy
   for the
   end

72 her eyes
   sad
   filled
   with memories
   of time
   long passed
   a youth
   of rebellion
   widowed
   at seventeen
   a second union
   her soulmate
   companion
   father
   of her children
   cut short
   divided
   by faith

73 they talk
   voices
   loud
   rich
   with the syrupy
   accent
   of the south

74 they ponder
   the future
   of the old
   abandoned
   dairy queen
   they dream
   of seeing
   a real
   honest
   hitchin' post
   in its place
   with plenty
   of space
   for a herd
   of mustangs
   four legged
   and ford

75 they conspire
   over bacon
   eggs
   on the status
   of things
   politics
   the world

76 they reflect
   on lives
   long since retired
   from dark mornings
   ranching
   rising
   before the sun
   herding
   cattle
   by starlight
   orion
   for a guide

77 her innocence
   lust
   for life
   hunger
   for stories
   eager
   to learn
   everything
   she can
   about who
   i am

78 her smile
   warm
   overflowing
   with love
   giddy excitement
   shining
   through

79 her every word
   spoken
   quickly
   as if racing
   to be sure
   nothing
   is left
   unsaid

80 she lacks
   concern
   for what others
   may think
   of her
   unabashed
   excitement
   joy
   adoration
   faith

81 she was born
   without the filter
   that disturbs
   the honesty
   of most
   her words
   those of truth

82 she grasps my hand
   her long
   lithe fingers
   chilled
   fragile
   knuckles
   like stones
   engulfed
   by my own
   fleshy palm

83 we sit
   together
   secure
   comfortable
   in our
   silence
   thoughts
   unspoken
   yet understood
   this strong
   steadfast
   woman
   i've only
   just met

84 they serenade
   each other
   off key
   tune
   tone
   rhythm
   lyrics
   created
   in the moment
   oblivious
   to the patrons
   the conversations
   they drown
   out

85 they talk
   of memories
   experiences
   had
   as a group
   a family
   of strangers
   brought together
   by faith
   unwavering
   devotion
   to the prophesies
   desires
   of a man
   believing himself
   to be
   god

86 he smuggles
   my wine
   in a to go
   soup bowl
   sensing
   recognizing
   without a word
   exchanged
   my exhaustion
   anxiety
   with the crowd

87 they gather
   encircling me
   like moths
   to a flickering
   slowly
   dimming
   dying
   candle
   flame
   drawn
   by a force
   unnamed
   unintentionally
   exuded

88 he's a barber
   the barber
   in a one
   stop light town
   a die hard
   rolling stone fan
   traversing
   the globe
   england
   brazil
   amsterdam
   allowing the spoils
   of his labors
   to sprinkle
   the floor
   opting to sip
   instead of sweep
   making it wiser
   to visit
   before
   noon

89 we're running
   away
   from the world
   responsibilities
   taxes
   neighbors
   to an island
   deserted
   lawless
   disconnected
   decadently
   our own

90 we were young
   teens
   fascinated
   with the dream
   fantasy
   of being
   desired
   by a man
   more mature
   experienced
   dangerous
   than the boys
   we knew

9I i leave behind
poor life
choices
unhealthy
decisions
regrets

i leave behind
time
spent
for others
too distracted
self
obsessed
to spend time
on me

i leave behind
relationships
maintained
for no reason
aside
from the fear
of cutting
ties

i leave behind
the habit
urge
to always
whisper
yes
when i want
nothing more
than to
shout
no

2 we drink
   coffee
   rewriting
   the lyrics
   to popular songs
   recrafting them
   at the top
   of our lungs
   to be
   our own
   sober
   yet buzzing
   with giddy
   energy
   childlike
   delight
   amusement

93 3 am
    with a snap
    i'm tugged
    back
    into existence
    no longer
    drifting
    amid rem level
    figments
    with a snap
    the jaws
    close
    new hesitation
    regret
    remorse
    signaling the end
    of our battle
    the intrusive
    rodent
    and i

94   they say
    you're
    gone
    the cause
    a patch
    of ice
    misplaced
    along the star
    lighted
    road
    unexpected
    uncontrolled
    unbelievable
    unfair
    unable to be
    undone

they say
you're
gone
no longer
smiling
a toothy
grin
creepy
on anyone
everyone
else
endearing
paired
with your signature
eyebrow
twitch

they say
you're
gone
body
broken
tossed
through
the window
like ash
no longer
glowing
with life

95 i felt it
when you
left
awoke
pulled
from slumber
by the absence
of sound
the missing
vibration
of your heart
no longer
beating
contributing
to the rhythm
of the world
i know

96 so young
twenty-five
the ink
not yet dried
on her degree
pursuing
embarking
on the path
winding
ahead
cut short
without warning
a dead-end
reached
no chance
of stalling
negotiating
changing lanes
a life
that will remain
unlived

97 i saw her
     there
     at the side
     of the road
     her hair
     blowing
     her body
     turned
     away
     from traffic
     the biting
     evening
     breeze
     hovering
     causing a jolt
     slamming brakes
     missing her
     body
     by a breath

98 i watch
     my rearview mirror
     finding it
     empty
     lacking
     the woman
     now
     gone
     only a figment
     a shadow
     of time
     a life
     an impression
     left
     from
     before

99 the sky turns
    to water
    color
    across the expanse
    of space
    the hills
    mountains
    trees
    no more than
    cardstock
    cutouts
    shapes
    shadows
    leftover
    scraps
    from a child's
    art project

100 the things
     we crave
     while the world
     around us
     crashes
     down
     ramen noodles
     cage free eggs
     black beans
     tortilla chips
     popcorn
     salty and sweet
     the shelves sit
     barren
     like those of old
     mother hubbard
     mocking me
     for my naive
     procrastination

IOI the mass
a hulking force
capable of taking
life
appearing
from within
the black
night
existing
audibly
long after
disappearing
into
the abyss

I02 he reads
the great
divorce
as i watch
the flames
of our humble
spring fire
his voice
illuminating
the dusk
of twilight

I03 i walk
with purpose
down aisles
once stocked
now picked
clean
devoured
by the community's
gluttonous
fear

I04 she stops me
a woman
her skin creased
with maturity
her hair
silver
frazzled
with experience
she needs
to speak
to interact
a reminder
that she isn't
alone

I05 spring
     finally
     the same season
     as every year
     before
     but different
     now
     in so many ways
     the sun
     shines
     blooms of color
     burst
     birds chirp
     greeting
     the morning sun
     deer venture
     further
     back into the world
     too long
     inhabited
     by man
     now relinquished back
     to nature

I06 we're in this
     together
     the signs
     all read
     but are we
     really
     it feels much more
     akin
     to our being
     all in this
     alone

I07 how is it that
     in times of strain
     we strike out
     biting
     clawing
     pushing
     others
     further down
     below
     our own
     misery
     uncertainty
     fear
     choosing hate
     over love
     losing
     our
     humanity

I08 it's catching
spreading
like wildfire
a blatant
disregard
disrespect
disgust
for our fellow
man

I09 i can't say
that all lives
matter
that attraction
to children
is a crime
not
a sexuality
that a privilege
is different
than a right
or a genetic trait

by thinking
these thoughts
by making
these statements
aloud
i'm labeled
a racist
a bigot
a closed minded
fool

I10 fear
causing us to strike
out
bite
challenge
condemn
strangers
unlucky enough
to exist

III they hum
hovering
close
whispering
their secrets
dastardly
plans
of world domination
one bite
at a time

II3 their feet
shuffle
weary
gnarled
from decades
spent
carrying
their bodies
through life
with purpose
intent
devotion
experiencing
all
the world has
to offer

II2 it's shocking
unnerving
so foreign
to drive
down a quiet
dimly lit
street
through the old
historic district
frozen
in an era
long past
men
clad in black
camouflaged
by the night
their intentions
displayed
clearly
without question
by their weapons
brandished
serving
their neighbors
protecting
their property
freedom
livelihood
life

POST CARD

This Space for Writing Messages

For address only

Place
Stamp Here

Domestic
One cent
Foreign
Two cents

4 happiness is
   ending the day with fish scales
   on the tips of my fingers
   radiating vitamin d
   from the apples of my cheeks
   wind blown sea spray
   filling my lungs & hair
   a smile courtesy the fresh memory
   of observing a woman
   patiently waiting
   for her friends
   to turn their attention
   towards a random piece of flotsam
   she'd proclaimed to be a whale
   sneakily emptying the contents
   from their tumblers of wine
   into her own
   well played, blanche
   well played

II5 i'm in love
     i tell you
     for the first time
     in my 36 years
     i'm in love
     never get married
     you tell me
     it's all arguing
     broken promises
     ignoring
     the unsaid
     settling
     for less

II6 sweet
    dry
    ice cold with only enough bubbles
    to tickle the tongue
    it goes down
    easily
    smooth
    too easily perhaps
    liquid courage
    easing through my veins
    inhibitions sparking
    from the tips of my fingers
    it's going to be a good night

II7 tension
    fear
    anxiety
    anticipation
    all eased
    while your smile curved lips
    brush against my own
    oxytocin fueled breath
    shared
    a meeting
    of your spirit with mine
    no hesitation
    question
    insecurity
    unanswered
    by a kiss
    that's only the beginning

II8　rough white guide
　　braille
　　serving to divide
　　here
　　from there
　　road
　　from ravine

II9　i pray
　　your intent
　　was pure
　　only confused
　　convoluted
　　in its execution
　　meant not
　　to harm
　　destroy
　　your true message
　　simply lost
　　in translation

I20　looking up
　　into the midnight blue of the clear night sky
　　through the ghastly haze of the smoke
　　from my crackling fire
　　warming my toes & providing a smooth cover
　　to the thrill of the train whistle
　　announcing its crossing
　　the points of the big dipper
　　thumbtacks holding the heavens in place
　　winking softly - confirming their presence
　　dimming with the passion of a hurried plane
　　or ufo
　　i've lain here
　　like this
　　every spring for 35 years
　　watching - waiting - for a shooting star
　　for my chance
　　to make a wish

I2I the soft buzz
     of the power lines
     a lullaby
     familiar from my youth
     like that of the engine's siren
     announcing a fire
     no longer intentional
     serving to clear
     sunday drivers from their path

I22 happiness is
     relaxing into the soft threads
     of a time worn quilt
     the crisp scent of dew dusted grass
     wafting on the breeze
     laseresque rays of vitamin d
     breaking through the clouds
     seeking their target
     amidst my ink-stained
     albino shell
     awakened from my reverie
     by the tickle of a ladybug
     meandering on her journey
     across my forearm
     bound for whatever
     undiscovered treasures
     may lie beyond

I23 the tea stained face
     of the main in the moon
     watching over
     the world below
     while jupiter hangs
     as if caught in the web
     of an astronomical arachnid

I24 i read a blog today
     about men preferring
     debt free virgins without tattoos
     the author
     if we're calling her that
     detailed how college debt
     sexual promiscuity
     headstrong independence
     all rival a woman's place
     with a husband
     a home
     happiness

     i have debt
     from exploring the globe
     a degree studying social & criminal injustices
     independence - sweet independence
     tattoos that would make a biker proud
     a home
     happiness

     happiness, dear lori, is not one size fits all

I25   never buy candy apples
     from witches
     reading makes my head
     feel full
     a hypothesis is a good guess
     with science

     i often wonder
     why we don't pay more attention
     to the wisdom
     coming
     from the mouths of babes

     (quotes courtesy my 9 year old nephew)

                      I26 sherbet colored walls
                           surround us
                           giggling like teens
                           within this room
                           surely haunted
                           by the remnants
                           of questionable
                           characters
                           who've come
                           before

I27 i say yes
     to new experiences
     memories
     relationships
     lessons
     adventures

     i say yes
     to reconnecting
     with myself
     my story
     voice
     present
     future

     i say yes
     to silences
     filled not with awkwardness
     but hope
     and the buzz
     of new beginnings

I28 i wonder does god ever
     regret
     weapons
     hate
     anger
     obsession
     organized religion
     free will

I29　i've never before
woken
ensconced in fear
that someone
you
might awake
and realize
that i'm not the one

but your tender kiss
strong touch
passion
adoration
love
are worth
every bated breath

I30　when i was little
i thought the rain
were tears
from god
i wonder now
if my imaginings
were closer
to the truth
than common sense
has made me believe

I3I　at what point
does the real me cease to exist
my personality - no longer mine
but instead that of the being you've created
by trimming away the parts
that offend
that question
challenge
that stand out - and stand up
the parts that are me
and not you
the parts i treasure most

I32   the incessant chatter
      of the flock
      sharing the latest gossip
      loud enough for all to hear
      resonating off the surface
      of the softly rippling bay
      pausing only briefly
      to take a bite
      of whatever remnants were left
      behind
      by the tourists
      who fled
      unable to keep up
      with the local news

I33   curled awkwardly in the back of my car
      craning our necks
      to see the screen
      the film
      meant for children
      failing to serve as a distraction
      from your kiss
      instead
      turning us both into giddy teens
      sneaking away
      for a night
      under the stars
      giggling with embarrassment
      excitement
      with every inquiring strangers stare

I34 the chimes
     hanging solemn & mute
     for so many weeks
     waking me this morning
     with the subtlest of sounds
     touched ever so slightly
     by an unseen breeze
     a welcome sign of reprieve
     from the smoke
     so seamlessly blanketing
     my corner of the world
     a signal for all listening
     that fall is near

                          I35 at what point
                               does breath
                               cease to be
                               weighted
                               by life
                               no longer possessed
                               by a soul
                               exhaled
                               in relief
                               disgust
                               resignation
                               and become
                               only
                               air

36 a harvest moon - the result of light
    scattered by the earth's atmosphere
    its color
    a spooky reminder of fall
    the thinning of the veil
    between
    living and dead
    what does it mean though
    when it's a harvest sun
    brightness muted
    by the haze of smoke
    wafting from flames
    here below
    the color of strawberries
    summer ripened, juice filled & plucked
    from the vine
    perhaps
    the end is near

                    I37 children
                         savor your youth
                         no one reads you stories
                         or recommends naps
                         when you've grown up
                         and you crave
                         nothing more

138 what is love
     but the unfaltering acceptance
     of another
     no matter the difference
     or distance
     from your soul & theirs
     an appreciation of their life story
     lessons learned
     mistakes made
     genuine empathy & concern
     for the bump, bruises & scars
     on their heart
     and a willingness
     to share with them
     your own

                    139 an evening spent
                         under the stars
                         looking back
                         on the paths traveled
                         alone
                         before they crossed
                         merging into one
                         the glow of fireworks
                         the moon
                         casting a brilliant glow
                         coloring your smile
                         distracting me
                         from the nibbling
                         mosquitos
                         devouring me alive

140 fat girls don't get eating disorders
     their shape & jean size
     repercussions of a life lived
     wrong
     fat girls get to be funny
     to have pretty faces
     sparkling personalities
     stunning smiles

     fat girls don't have to worry
     about strangers
     spotting the bruises
     hidden on their hearts
     safe beneath the curves
     behind their smile

                    141 pumpkin
                         nutmeg
                         cinnamon
                         ginger
                         cloves
                         the spicy spirits of fall
                         permeating throughout
                         my kitchen
                         wafting from the oven
                         dancing atop my taste buds
                         stoking the flickering light
                         that reveals the darkest
                         corners of my hidden
                         creative depths

I42 my home
a sanctuary
an asylum
a resting place
a hideaway
my safe place
my escape away from the world
sacred
without outside
influences
people
until you
i give you the key
to my heart
to my home
an invitation
a plea
that you come inside

I43 the age old adage
the customer is always right
stops ringing true
when your entitlement
presumption
ignorance
rage
hate
spew forth from the curled lips
and forked tongue
of your foul mouth

44 a steady rhythm
   chopping
   dicing
   sweeping
   into the pan
   asparagus, bell pepper, spring onions,
   sugar peas, string beans
   a crisp healthy
   snap
   vibrant green in color & crunch
   a softly rippling boil of coconut milk
   the bite of chili & curry
   flavors of comfort & fall

                I45 you...
                    make me feel like dancing
                    complete me
                    make me want to be a better me
                    had me at hello
                    left your mark on me
                    were the one i tried to draw
                    reflect me
                    make me feel like a natural woman
                    fill me up
                    give me premature ventricular
                    contractions
                    should be kissed often
                    have bewitched me
                    body & soul

I46   i've always been
       a self proclaimed
       commitment-phob
       breaking out in hives
       chilly sweats
       goosedots
       at the very idea
       of spending more than
       a few hours
       with another
       but
       this overthinking
       failure fearing
       ocd perfectionist
       has no hesitation
       or pause
       when it comes to you

                                    I47   fall
                                           finds
                                           me
                                           falling
                                           in
                                           love

48 i ache
    from the guilt
    i feel
    over obligations
    to others

    i yearn
    to no longer
    be filled
    with a crippling
    fear
    of failure

    i dream
    of pursuing my own
    passions
    purpose
    possibilities
    without
    guilt
    fear

149 the last sliver
     of sunlight
     warmth
     cutting through
     the curtains
     leaving a trail
     of sun
     crumbs
     the remnants of
     summer
     fading away
     into the mist
     the rain
     of fall

150   thumb
       knuckle
       palm
       fist
       elbow
       heel
       steady progression of pain
       release
       relief
       muscles once so tightly wound
       now relaxed
       pliant
       like warm taffy
       twisted & pulled
       fluid & smooth

                    151   waking up to find you
                           waiting at my door
                           coffee cup in hand
                           arms outreached
                           eyes twinkling
                           appraising me
                           adoring me
                           with mussed hair
                           morning breath
                           eau'd'stomach flu
                           seeping from my pores
                           this much be
                           that which they call
                           love

I52   driving
      pondering
      the origin of
      every meandering
      curve
      as we climb
      the tree shadowed
      hillside
      of these moss green
      dormant volcanoes
      contemplating
      if they might not be
      giants
      snoozing
      for eternity
      voices hushed
      so as not to disturb
      their slumber

I53   the chimes tinkle
      the music box plays
      no breath of wind
      no touch of hand
      shadows shift
      movements recalled
      long after
      the end

I54   words
      fill me
      humble me
      intrigue me
      challenge me
      posses me
      enrapture me

I55   autumn leaves
      littering the asphalt
      brightly colored
      stars
      fallen
      from the tree tops
      above

her name is linda
the petite asian woman
silently vanquishing the knots
in my shoulders
neck
back
hips
her silence broken
with the tiniest of laughs
at the moment she glimpses
my grandfather
his west point graduation portrait
residing on my outer thigh
facial massage for you sir
she whispers
i tell linda
she's relieved the tension
worked magic
on my body
and soul

157 do you ever
    close your eyes
    throw back your head
    and listen
    for the sounds
    of the stars
    the electric crackling
    as they hover in space
    time
    tugging
    feverishly
    at the invisible strings
    holding them
    in place
    striving to shoot
    across the sky

158 how long
    does one wait
    before broaching
    marriage
    you asked me
    awaiting my answer
    with
    bated
    breath

159 your heart
    calls to mine
    in a language
    at a frequency
    never before
    known

PLACE POSTAGE STAMP HERE

POST CARD

THE ADDRESS TO BE WRITTEN ON THIS SIDE

THIS SIDE FOR CORRESPONDENCE

U.S.A.

543

160 our fingers
     entwined
     resting on my thigh
     your eyes
     attention
     on the twisting
     road ahead
     laughing aloud
     at the silliest
     of things
     our demeanor
     that of worry-free
     youth
     moments like these
     ours alone
     yet another reason
     i love you

161 religion
     is funny
     often
     dictating
     opinions
     actions
     providing hope
     measured
     in doses
     deemed
     harmless enough
     so as to not
     tempt
     the chosen

162 i woke this morning
     in a panic
     my heart
     racing
     my head
     aching
     completely overtaken
     with the realization
     i don't necessarily like
     the person
     i've become

I63 the night sky
     devoid of moon or stars
     seeping into the shadows
     of the mountains
     surrounding
     this twisting road
     scarred across the hillside
     ensconced by trees
     their evergreen hue
     now void & noir
     my heart
     skips a beat
     my reflective trail of breadcrumbs
     disappears
     into nothing
     at every turn   I64 she sits back
     as if i'm destined   relaxed completely
     to follow blindly   into the fabric
     into the night   of her chair
                              hair disheveled
                              glasses cocked
                              arms moving
                              rapidly
                              painting
                              an image
                              across the space
                              before her
                              comfortable
                              confident
                              unapologetic
                              real

I65 our obsession
     addiction
     to experience the world
     by observing
     the experiences
     of others
     strangers
     living lives
     not always so different
     than our own
     were we only
     to give ourselves
     permission
     encouragement
     time
     freedom
     to explore
     to live

                    I66 9 days
                         2I6 hours
                         spent adventuring
                         exploring
                         getting lost
                         together
                         finding myself
                         falling more and more
                         in love
                         with you
                         and i
                         at every
                         turn

I67 my grandmother died
9 months before i was
born
drowned
suicide
not her first
attempt
i've always felt her
watching
from the exposed frame
doorway of the kitchen
a shadow
hidden
at the edge
of my sight

I68 the tlingit believe
the souls of the lost
drowned
are tempted
transfixed
transformed
rebirthed
to live again
as a frolicking sea otter
kushtaka
hauntingly comforting
for those of us
who've lost someone
to the sea

169 the sound of the waves
crashing into the shore
followed by the
crackling
clicking
clacking
as it tumbles
polishes
the stones
caught in its wake
until they're smooth
as silk
no longer
able to resist
its pull

170 jets
perched on the tarmac
like gulls
tucked in
for the night

171 iron tracks from lifetimes before
     wind along the hillside
     below
     following the reflective guidelines of the road
     the mountains & foothills framing my sight
     not majestically blue
     like home
     but gold
     amber
     bronze
     rustic in their unfettered beauty
     untouched
     untainted
     exactly as they're meant to be
     woody & rough
     unapologetic
     real

                172 128
                     the number of train cars
                     careening
                     just outside the reach
                     of my fog dimmed head lights
                     the number of days
                     we've been together
                     that you've been mine
                     and i
                     yours

173 we curl together
a quilt filled with goose down
tethering us to the bed
your legs
entwined with mine
not unlike a cephalopod
arms twisting
cradling each other
nearly impossible to determine
where one ends
and the other
begins

174 i read
a russian fairytale
dark
romantic   175 he sings
vexing   in the shower
you snooze   he holds
your breath   my hand
steady   he kisses
measured   my forehead
while the winter storm   he smiles
pummels   with his eyes
the paneled glass   he fills
above our heads   my heart

I76 the mountains
     their massive shapes
     towering
     commanding
     but muted
     softened
     by the falling
     rain

                    I77 the moon casts its eerie glow
                         on the wisps of clouds
                         hiding the twinkling
                         of the stars
                         its form
                         bisected
                         the man
                         only half
                         of who he was
                         before
                         reminiscent of
                         melpomene
                         missing thalia

178 the fat drops
      falling
      composing
      a rhythmic
      beat
      a tribal
      chant
      on the hollow logs
      above our heads

179 your passion shows
      with sizzling bacon
      cubed potatoes
      diced shallots
      fresh clams
      a silky roux
      3 parts heavy cream
      butter
      flour
      passion
      love

180 the gull's cries
      echo
      resounding
      amongst the spindly legs
      of the pier
      i wonder
      has she too sought solace
      here
      hiding
      away from the world
      working through the demons
      in her head

I8I our hands fit
    joints
    digits
    fingers
    palms
    as if formed
    from the same clay
    flesh
    electrified
    with the same
    current

I82 he sings
    in the shower
    an eclectic mix of
    italian opera
    50s do wop
    original compositions
    cat food commercials
    this
    is love

I83 stars shine
    bright
    a statement of strength
    perseverance
    against the powerful
    cobalt sky
    not yet overshadowed
    by the coral light
    of dawn
    visible through the naked limbs
    of the frost bitten trees
    speckling the field

I84 i sit here
    sipping coffee
    watching the sun
    tickling
    teasing
    the frost
    from the naked tree tops
    i wait
    for the ice to warm
    melt
    disappear
    from the windshield
    of my humble suv

I85 she stumbles
    from the creaking
    collapsible
    aluminum steps
    of the rusted
    beige rv
    her drink of choice
    no longer bottled
    safely
    on a shelf
    instead
    surging
    through her veins

I86 when did things change
    the gravity defying shift
    from courtesy & compassion
    to malice & vehemence
    causing us to turn
    so quickly
    so brutally
    on one another
    attacking
    for no reason
    aside from
    desiring
    to bear witness
    to be the cause
    of another's demise

187 the spindly skeletal limbs
     sharpened like a knife
     fractured
     by frost
     only weeks ago
     shrouded in brilliant reds
     yellows
     now silver
     nature's camouflage
     any sign of life
     hibernating deep
     within the core
     waiting to re-emerge
     in spring

188 i burrow
     my face
     into the curve
     where your neck
     and shoulder   189 hiking atop
     meet   the glacier
     your chest   plates of ice
     breathing   formed long ago
     you in   a time
     losing   before
     myself   now
     in the rhythmic   not a creature
     pulsing   is stirring
     of your   not even
     heart   a moose

190 tiny
dark
papered completely
with salt air
crunched
dollar bills
the elbow weathered
bar
occupied by three souls
locals
oblivious
to the presence
of a stranger
in their midst

191 winter
is here
the trees
bare
fields
frosted
coffee
spiked
crock pots
filled

192 the spit
boarded up
abandoned
for the season
coney island
of the west coast
tiny shops
balance
precariously
atop stilts
solid
against the angry
waves
of winter

193 lately
i feel akin
to a bird
flying into
the wind
a salmon
fighting
the current
swimming
upstream
both driven
and challenged
by nature

I94   he notices
     the little things
     my nail polish
     hair color
     eye lashes
     earrings
     freckles
     dimples
     he notices
     me

I95   mandala's theory
     of neighborly
     hate
     distrust
     dislike
     appears stronger
     now
     amidst the season
     of peace
     hope
     love

I96   it's empowering
     personally
     quietly
     making the decision
     choosing the intention
     to shift
     from following
     the norm
     always focused
     on bolstering a resume
     meant to impress
     faceless strangers
     to instead
     accomplish feats that will last
     beyond
     my time on earth
     filling the lines
     of a eulogy
     meant to comfort
     those i've loved

197 spindly
     skeletal
     exposed
     dancing
     stripped bare
     by the wind

198 lying here
     my cheek pressed
     against your chest
     legs entwined
     our bodies
     without a breath
     between us
     unable to move
     for the weight
     of the winter quilt
     the world
     the cat
     the dog

199 a winter evening
     spent cocooned
     in layers
     of fleece blankets
     held in place
     by the love
     in your arms
     warming me
     from within

200 it's been three months
     without the scent
     of fresh cut grass
     sunshine
     coconut oil
     slathered bodies
     instead
     the air is crisp
     clear
     tainted with just a
     hint
     of wood smoke
     summoning
     dreams of snow

201 people swoon
over puppy breath
but for me
it isn't the breath
or the puppy
it's the smooth area of skin
devoid of all fur
hidden just between
the ear
and smile
of my nine year old
terrier's cheek
that eases my stress
calms my nerves
and brings me back
home

202 the feeling of
discomfort
pain
persecution
spending ones life
knowing
the endless cycle of stress
anxiety
surrounding you
is far too quickly
silently
killing your spirit
passion
fire
purpose

203 no longer
   will i kill myself
   draining
   every bit of energy
   life
   focus
   drive
   in the pursuit
   of someone else's
   purpose
   beginning now
   i reclaim my time
   passion
   intent
   wanderlust
   my life
   as my own

204 i dream
   of existing
   in the world
   locked safely
   within
   my head
   heart
   imagination

205 i'm addicted
   to your passions
   your smile
   your fingers
   as they trace the
   curve
   of my face
   your intellect
   your interests
   your moments
   of unrestrained
   laughter
   your scent
   your patience
   your passion
   i'm contentedly
   addicted
   to you

206 life is
    precious
    fleeting
    fragile
    to be lived
    loved
    enjoyed
    ridden hard
    exhausted
    devoured
    to the very
    last
    drop

207 it's unexpectedly
    spectacularly
    unexplainably
    fantastic
    the easy way
    you seem to read
    my thoughts
    dreams
    hesitations
    obsessions
    without my having
    to say
    a word

208 lying here
    my head
    resting
    on a pillow
    in your lap
    your fingers
    tracing shapes
    along my scalp
    the length
    of my hair
    sliding between
    i know now
    why dogs
    wag their tails

209 your scent
    fresh
    male
    with the slightest
    hint
    of tobacco
    uniquely
    you
    lingers
    on the sheets
    fills my lungs
    my heart

2I0 this morning
i watched
as a woman said farewell
to her four legged companion
burying her face
into the downy fur of his collar
holding him close
whispering words
of love
gratitude
grief
i watched
as her two legged companion
cursed & chastised her
for making a decision
he could not

2II it's exhausting
the endless pursuit
of perfection
always knowing
somewhere
deep within
that perfection
is
impossible
that i'll always be
imperfect
just shy
of good
enough

212 i'm working on being
     completely vulnerable
     with myself
     vocalizing my fears
     concerns
     worries
     putting them out
     into the universe
     opening myself
     to any support
     clarity
     i may receive
     from the universe
     god
     or whomever it is
     that may be listening

213 you wax poetic
     over the loss
     of
     your foreskin
     taken
     without your permission
     long before
     you'd found
     your voice
     i can't help myself
     laughing
     to the point
     of tears

2I4 i watched
     through the rain speckled glass
     as your head dipped
     below the ledge
     of your trash littered dashboard
     reappearing
     moments later
     frantically wiping
     remnants of white powder
     from the tip of your nose
     i watched
     as you chose
     a quick fix
     placing your own high
     over the needs of the small
     innocent
     child
     dreaming
     behind you

                        2I5 her tail
                             twitches
                             a metronome
                             keeping time
                             with the rhythmic purrs
                             rumbling
                             from deep within
                             her core

2I6 3 letters
printed black
affixed to the
remnants
of a once white cross
weather worn
beaten grey
by the exhaust
of countless others
passing too quickly
to notice
3 letters
a life
a story
dad

2I7 you're stronger
than you feel
more brilliant
than you believe
still innocent
untainted
by the world
outside
i pray
you remain
pure
honest
true
to you

2I8 the feathers
flutter
ever so slightly
no longer
moving
with breath
but at the insistence
of the wind

2I9 you're beautiful
in a pierced
dimple
punk rock
substance dealing
parolee
porcelain doll
type of way

220 when the odds
      are stacked
      against you
      the world
      spinning
      faster
      than your legs
      can manage
      the expectations
      greater
      than ever imagined
      in the darkest
      depths
      of your
      prepubescent
      fears
      the best prescription
      is often as simple
      as a crispy
      golden
      grilled
      cheese

22I that's
      like
      super
      dope
      he says
      with confidence
      a response
      i can't begin
      to understand
      this child
      sitting before me
      ensconced within
      the body
      of a man

222 ring around
      the man
      in the moon
      crimson in color
      against a dusky
      grey
      sky
      speckled
      with stars
      my arms
      prickle
      with remembered
      warnings
      of blood
      doom

POST CARD

For Address Only.

For Correspondence.

"Snowflake" Series-Christmas-Postcard No. 1204. Printed in Vienna.

223 i often wonder
    how the scene appeared
    to the chicken
    pecking eagerly
    the minuscule grass shoots
    struggling toward the sun
    along the edge of the sparkling glass
    serving to keep her out
    amongst the living world
    and us in
    with the casket
    and our grief

224 a split second
    captured
    with the flash
    of a bulb
    9 cousins
    unfamiliar
    strangers
    connected only
    by blood
    posed
    along the cold
    backdrop
    of a carved
    wooden bench
    forced smiles
    laughter
    nervous fidgeting
    innocence
    frozen
    in time

225 it's been a decade
and a half
since i last knelt
at the alter
accepting
forgiveness
grace
a fresh start
from a man
empowered
by god
acting
in his jest
yet i feel more
balanced
renewed
clear than ever before
sitting here
watching the waves
splash the shore

226 it seems
you can read me
like a picture
book
anytime
i'm pondering
contemplating
sharing thoughts
aloud
you nearly take
the words
from off my
tongue
it's spooky
fantastic
for the first
time
i feel seen
heard
understood
accepted
loved

227 she used the paper
    napkin
    only a moment ago
    so crisp
    pure
    to smooth back
    his sweaty
    pomade lathered
    locks
    thinner than before
    more transluscent
    than in his youth
    hiding perhaps
    in the recesses
    of a skullcap
    long ago
    retired

228 lessons learned
    time served
    mistakes lived
    hidden pieces
    of why you are
    who you are
    today

229 i'm sad
    i was fixing
    the world
    but
    they woke me up
    before i could
    finish

    *anesthetic
    murmurings
    of the man
    i love*

230 your bruises
    so carefully
    hidden
    beneath
    your unblemished
    alabaster
    façade

231 burrowing my
    fingers
    my face
    into the thick
    fur
    of your collar
    breathing in
    your unrestrained
    spirit
    you breathe
    panting
    against my cheek
    ears perked
    anticipating
    the call
    of your pack

232 the snow falls
    soft
    sifted flour
    filtered
    through
    clouds
    colanders
    resting
    where it lies
    kissing
    just the tip
    of the trees
    your nose

233 i listen
    as she speaks
    of cancer
    dying
    honestly
    on her own terms
    but first
    of leaving
    her essence
    here
    for her daughters

234 the hills
mountains
a patchwork
quilt
designs
etched by frost
snow
animal tracks
some four legged
some two
all seeking shelter
from the cold

236 i love
eavesdropping
on the
conversations
of old men
long retired
concerned
with the
weather
anxiously
pacing
in wait
of their shot
at this week's
shuffleboard
title

235 wednesday nights
find us
in one of many
local watering
holes
intentionally
darkened
to elicit
encourage
foster
questionable
decisions
watching
chuckling
at the choices
of our peers

237 each member
of the pack
with a
personality
unique
as a fingerprint
ingrained
by nature
nurtured
by the wild

238 still a child
by most standards
only 9 months
of life
lived
experienced
but already
a predator
a natural force
a spirit
of the wild

239 i should know
by now
that passion
is more important
than perfection
that over-
planning
mutes magic
that life
isn't fair
and that love
is a battlefield

240 ripe avocados
extra fine ink pens
oversized sweaters
stiletto manicures
genuine sourdough
toasted with cheese
these are a few
of my favorite
things

24I the silence
uncomfortable
wrapped around
the city
a weighted
blanket
the world
disappearing
behind a curtain
of softly
falling
snow

242 fresh smashed guac
    gooey fudge brownies
    the fountainhead
    band of brothers
    blankets & pillows
    in excess
    even breathing
    tiny snores
    i'm unsure
    who fell asleep first
    you
    or the dog
    grown up snow days
    are my new favorite

243 it's magically
    hypnotic
    yet
    scientifically
    simple
    rain drops
    frozen
    no longer
    weightless
    balanced
    within the clouds

244 how is it
    something so
    simple
    snow
    can transform
    the angriest
    most tarnished
    scowl
    to a smile

245 you tell me
    i'm beautiful
    no prompting
    or eyelash
    fluttering
    a statement
    under your breath
    when i'm feeling
    unpretty
    and needing to
    hear it
    most

246 lights hang
    sadly forgotten
    remnants of
    celebrations
    long gone
    a season
    come and past

248 i've spent the
    day cleaning
    purging
    old obsessions
    once read books
    now sealed shut
    with age
    cobwebs strung
    corner to
    corner
    arachnid
    breadcrumbs
    for safe
    travels
    home
    material
    objects
    thought to hold
    memories
    emotions
    connections
    from the past

247 fields
    pure
    white
    with fresh snow
    untouched
    save the
    speckling
    of chattering
    blackbirds
    ducks
    geese
    breaking the
    early
    morning
    silence
    in their midst
    a lone hawk
    seeking to share
    their warmth

249 surrounded by snow
    we verbalized
    our decision
    to weave together
    our living spaces
    our finances
    our future adventures
    our stores
    our lives
    we started with a pair
    of avocado pits
    awaiting the first
    signs
    of life
    spring
    with bated breath
    anticipation
    joy

250 my first car was
    red
    like a cherry
    that's spent time
    in the long grass
    of an overgrown
    pasture
    nudged by the
    hooves
    of a wild mustang

251 i'm not mad
    or angry
    i'm disgusted
    fuming
    appalled
    by your utter
    disregard
    dismissal
    negligence
    of situations
    individuals
    responsibilities
    expectations
    commitments
    i'm saddened
    by you
    for you
    your comfort
    complacence
    with the lack
    of humanity
    you possess

252 it's not you
    it's me
    my innate desire
    to be
    in motion
    never setting
    still
    for fear
    of growing
    complacent
    missing
    the adventures
    destined
    to be mine

    it's not you
    your constant need
    for attention
    recognition
    praise
    it's me
    my constant need
    for independence
    quiet
    peace

253 let us recognize
the difference
between right & wrong
and possess the
gumption
to choose wisely

let us respect
our elders
heed their warnings
admire
their accomplishments
encourage
their independence

let us worship
freely
without judgement
persecution

let us use
our voices
for spreading truth
strength

let us remember
that childhood is short
innocence
priceless
naivete
fleeting

let us never
lose the thrill
of pumping
our legs
on a playground
swing
with the smallest
hope
of gaining
flight

let us be
open
eager
to love
one another
despite
our flaws

let us live
a life
of countless
memories
shared
adventures
no
regrets

254 strangers
having only learned
the others name
moments before
we sit together
worlds apart
the two of us
in this room
large enough
for a crowd
claustrophobic
with the weight
presence
of your confessions
lies
untruths
delusions
the web of stories
you weave

255 we were both
still
children
teens
struggling
to make sense
of our bodies
feelings
emotions
you professed
your lust
with words
that my young
yearning
ears
heard
as love

256 there must be
something
wrong
with me
i yearn
for the quiet
time alone
without the mask
required
by the world

257 just breathe
a reminder
posted everywhere
anywhere
bumpers
journals
tee shirts
why
put so much
focus
on something
our body does
without intent
reminded
by nature

258 i thrive
in the silence
the clarity
of a space
no longer weighted
by the stories
hopes
desires
woes
of others
devoid of
expectations
obligations

259 i watch you
your movements
body language
while you watch
the wall
avoiding eye contact
connection
that may threaten
to break
your mask
character
scene

260 i feel like a voyeur
eavesdropping
on the misadventures
heartbreaks
confessions
of strangers
via the recorded
snippets
they've shared
with the world

261 i wish
i could just
let go
of caring
too much
i envy
those able to remain
uninvested
concerned only
with their own
well being
unbothered
by the struggles
of others

262 i'm envious
of their courage
vulnerability
the ability
to share
such personal stories
struggles
failures
scars
with the public
shedding all layers
armor
inviting strangers
in
to observe
judge

263 weeks ago
   a rodent claimed
   spring was coming
   and yet
   here i sit
   burrowed within
   my cocoon of blankets
   i doze
   to the technicolor
   flames
   and unnatural
   crackling
   of a man made
   fireplace
   streaming
   from a screen
   as the snow falls
   outside

264 we sit
   giddy & smiling
   amidst
   a smattering of
   delicacies
   all foreign
   to us
   we chuckle
   as your chopsticks
   bounce
   atop a chilled
   boiled egg
   you watch my face
   as i contemplate
   a sliver of kimchi
   we observe
   as our fellow
   patrons
   feast
   with poise
   grace
   expertise
   and i fall
   in love with you
   all over again

265   i cry
      when you shock me
      with words
      of praise
      recognition
      thanks

      i cry
      when you question
      my passion
      dedication
      focus

      i cry
      without sound
      resigning myself
      to these truths
      dying to find
      a way to change
      who i am
      how i am

      i cry
      when you tell me
      i'm strong
      i'm worthy
      i'm making a difference
      i'm taking it too personal
      i'm too close

266 i perch here
    atop a long felled tree
    its trunk
    no longer
    standing proud
    having sacrificed itself
    as tribute
    to foster the new growth
    along the moss carpeted
    forest floor

267 i find comfort
    in the cycle
    surrounding us
    all
    elders
    submitting themselves   268 crab
    to the next   apple
    generation   cherry
    hoping   blossoms
    that next time   fragrant
    we just may   spring
    get it right   snow

269   the first
      sunny day
      dares me
      to hope
      that winter
      is over
      that spring
      with fresh breezes
      robins egg skies
      may be
      on its way

            270   from the corner of my eye
                  the blurred edge of my vision
                  i watch
                  with bated breath
                  as your monochromatic form
                  tall
                  slender
                  unquestionably male
                  steps away from the forest edge
                  separating itself
                  from the shadows
                  i turn
                  knowing you'll have vanished
                  but knowing still
                  i have to look
                  to try
                  to catch you
                  watching over me

271 i sit
steeped
in wonder
at the conversations
surrounding me
chirps
whispers
cries
hums
chatterings
without interpretation
i know
they too
are celebrating
spring

272 strangers
refusing to cross
the unspoken line
only serving
to further distance
us
from
each other

273 i wish
i'd met you sooner
to not have missed
squandered
a moment of life
with you
and yet i know
that we are
today
exactly who we need to be
for ourselves
for each other
for us
forever

274 i've never been
comfortable
asking
for help
showcasing
my flaws
inviting others
to observe
my vulnerabilities
until now

275 the last remnants
physical cues
of winter
trickle
from the mountain
white
pure
disappearing
before reaching
the foothills
below

276 from my space here
legs dangling
off the tailgate
my face
turned
to the sun
staining
my otherwise alabaster
skin
with the pink hue
of spring

277 my attention
focus
divided
between two stories
one
inked upon paper
held in my hands
the other
unfolding
with the chattering
wildlife
burgeoning
blossoms
of spring
ferns
surrounding me

278 water
falls
drops
tears
streaming
from the earth
physical manifestations
of mother nature's
happiness
of another year
springing
to life

279 seed pods
bursting
popping
with the heat
of the long awaited
springtime sun
new life
leaping forth
then settling
to start
roots
claiming a space
of their own

280 feet planted
shoulders rolled
back
your father's
russian pistol
formed the same year
as he
settled in my grasp
i fire
in the direction
of an offending
water bottle
my inexperience
granting it clemency
to exist
another day

281 mother nature's
cobwebs
curtains
intricately woven
moss
draping
dripping
from every
outstretched
limb
creating
a sense of privacy
seclusion
protection

POST ‡ CARD.

THE ADDRESS ONLY TO BE
WRITTEN HERE.

282 i can't be
the only
adult
who still finds
it simpler
less messy
to contemplate
life's most perplexing
conundrums
from here
within
the sanctuary
of a shared
blanket fort

283 we stand
hands clasped
breath
held
in silence
memorian
amidst the wreckage
ruins
remnants
of a hospital
meant to cure
in reality
a shame filled home
for those
held prisoner
by their mind

284 i'm terrified
you'll notice
the cracks
fissures
in my facade
the strong
unshakeable mask
i show
the world
and find
the scared
girl inside

285 so many souls
buried
abandoned
left
behind
here
in a field
marked
by a number
initials
so many lives
ignored
stories
untold

286 i love you
for the way
you explore
the ordinary
with me
pausing to wonder
at the mundane
wondering
at the choices
made
by our fellow man

287 i'm fearful
that you'll realize
you can do better
deserve better
want better
than me

288 I2 hours meandering
    towards a destination
    going
    our own way
    a drive that others complete
    in 4
    pausing to wander
    cemeteries
    to wonder
    at the ocean's waves
    as they crest
    crash
    into the southwestern
    most point
    of the state
    we call home

289 moss crusted
    cobblestones
    slick
    with the crystalline
    spray
    emanating
    from the overpowering
    falls

290 inscriptions
unique
etched with intent
by design
to give pause
a chuckle
a smirk
a tear
to commemorate
memorialize
a life
lived

292 voices
audible
only within
the confines
of her mind
thoughts
criticisms
opinions
threats
spouted forth
with malintent
from the mouths
of formless
imagined
beings

291 we watch
hearts
breaking
as she stumbles
along the street
edge
challenging
every passing car
driver
to end
the pain
turmoil
confusion
voices
to make it all
stop

293 knowing that if i
continue
to fight
to not
let go
i will
break
my mind
heart
belief
in the goodness
of man
kind

294 your face
is aglow
your smile
making it impossible
for me to not
imagine
you
as a child
we pass the home
where you grew up
the houses
of your oldest
friends
your partners
in crime
your life
before me

295 bynum, montana
dinosaur country
blackleaf ridge
the rocky mountains
we stand
in awe
speechless
at the majesty
magnificence
mysterious
perfection

296 the endless highway
seemingly disappears
over every rolling
hill
rematerializing
only when we've climbed
crested
the next
peak

they married as children
my mom & dad
he
fresh from the navy
making his way home
stateside
after years of adventure
sowing his oats
across europe
she
fresh from highschool
making her escape
from a life spent
abroad
the rebellious daughter
of a dictating colonel
both seeking
structure
stability
safety
peace

298 cape
disappointment
ironically
one of the most
awe inspiring
breath taking
locations
at the southwestern most
tip
of washington state
a disappointment
only
to those
seeking to
not
be humbled
at the vast majesty
of mother
nature

299 i find myself
here
in a field
miles wide
unfenced
bordered only
by the rocky mountains
surrounded
by a mooing herd
of cattle
a tumultuously passive
standoff
evoked by my harmless
attempt
at making friends
with one
of their tiniest
calves

300 we stand
in silence
surrounded
by wildlife
invisible
yet ever present
watching
nervously
hoping
to cross paths
with a recently
awakened
no longer
dozing
grizzly bear
to ask him
how he slept

30I family secrets
buried deep
below lies
stories
intentional avoidance
their weight
amplified
with every decade
passed
generations
laid to rest
often lost
never to be heard
explained
understood

302 you're wrong
    about me
    about the issue being
    that i care
    too much
    that i take
    my position
    my responsibilities
    my contributions
    too seriously
    that i give
    too many
    fucks
    about the well being
    of those
    in my employ
    you're wrong
    about everything
    but that doesn't
    make it right

303 i breathe you in
    your essence
    that of a man
    honest
    freethinking
    passionate
    selfless
    filling my nostrils
    throat
    lungs
    with who you are
    succumbing
    gladly
    to who i become
    who i am
    in your presence

304 it's always seemed
    like magic
    that fleeting moment
    between evening
    and dusk
    immeasurable
    inconsequential
    a breath
    of time
    an unseen switch
    flipped
    sparking street lights
    to life
    signaling
    day is done

306 i'm not used to this
    feeling
    of vulnerability
    anxiety
    hesitation
    unrest
    my entire being
    frozen
    in limbo
    waiting
    for one word
    your decision
    on my worth

305 spring sun
    at high noon
    a rainbow
    reflected
    on the shelled casing
    of a beetle's back

307 i dream
of waking
every morning
giddy
at the prospect
of what lies
ahead
proud
of my contributions
excited
by the projects
occupying my time
heart
mind
constantly
refilling
my cup

308 i'm meant to forage
pilfer & collect
stories of lifetimes
adventures
lessons
loves
losses
to share
educate
enrich
the knowledge
understanding
comprehension
of what was
what has been
for those
who're yet to be

309 strangers
whose lives are now
connected
a delicate web
of shared experience
having played voyeur
to the majesty
of nature
the breathtaking escapades
of gentle giants
so seldom seem

3I0 every year
    as winter eases
    into spring
    i'm drawn again
    into the world
    created
    with words
    on pages
    creased & torn
    faded with age
    sunlight
    spotted with coffee
    wine
    tears

3II my body
    is soft
    legs
    sturdy
    built
    to march
    dance
    entwine
    with yours
    breasts
    smooth
    naturally
    relaxed
    against
    the flesh cocoon
    of my ribcage

3I2 he has cancer
    she mouths
    barely a breath
    of sound
    escaping
    her overly
    exaggerated
    lips
    drawing out
    the word
    no longer 2
    short
    syllables
    but 4

3I3 the gigantic tails
    slip
    gracefully
    into the seams
    between waves
    without
    a sound
    no effort
    as if
    they were never
    here

314 i'd like to tell
    my future self
    to be proud
    of the risks
    taken
    to celebrate
    obstacles
    overcome
    relationships
    fostered
    and released
    to not regret
    or berate
    myself
    for the time it's taken
    to feel
    secure
    comfortable
    empowered
    in myself
    my strengths

315 i wish
    i wasn't
    afraid
    of failure
    rejection
    being labeled
    a disappointment
    not good
    enough

    i wish
    i was strong
    enough
    to tell you
    no
    bold enough
    to stand
    in your way
    to put a stop
    to the way
    you make me
    feel
    to take back
    my voice

3I6 the holiday weekend
    unfailingly
    tugging at
    reeling in
    the invisible cords
    tying those
    who were once
    classmates
    never
    friends
    now
    strangers
    back
    towards home

3I7 it's spring
    again
    i can tell
    by the cacophony
    of voices
    chattering
    chirping
    cricketing
    croaking
    bouncing
    echoing
    amongst
    the twinkling stars
    polka dotting
    the clear
    northwestern sky

3I8 his eyes stare
    blank
    yet loaded
    impossibly deep
    cavernous
    peering
    from within
    the wall
    judging
    those of us
    whose elbows smooth
    the bar
    beneath
    his gaze

3I9 i did a thing
    i made a choice
    to close the door
    on a career
    for which i've bled
    sweat
    cried
    a career
    that has not
    filled my cup
    stoked my fire
    teased my passion

320 i've made the
decision
to no longer
endure
my day to day
to give myself
permission
to live
to pursue
the crazed
sideways
dreams
i've stifled
far
too
long

32I the relief
every nerve
muscle
unwound
relaxed
for the first time
in four years
after telling you
i'll no longer
do your bidding
answer
to you
second guess
my heart
gut
morals
i quit

322 i'm not sure exactly
    when it happened
    that shift
    from my spending
    evenings
    devouring beverages
    to dull my emotions
    to soften
    the never ceasing
    demon
    angel
    that resides within
    to instead
    inebriate myself
    with the stories
    shared freely
    poured out
    by the strangers
    at my side

323 their voices blend
    like water & oil
    meeting
    exceeding
    with volume
    tenacity
    clashing
    at every note

324 we adventured south today
     fighting our natural tendencies
     to flee
     the helter skelter
     of the big city
     it's crowds
     entitled masses
     instead
     we followed
     the downstream flow of traffic
     into the cold heart
     of the city
     hiding away
     as best we could
     in a somewhat less
     crazed
     corner
     enjoying a meal
     each others company
     before rejoining the mad rush
     against the current
     back towards home
     sanctuary

325 we adventured north today
    crossing the border
    on an international mission
    to satisfy our mutual curiosity
    seeking a new cuisine
    an experience
    to awaken
    our tastebuds
    i shared with you
    dill pickle & ketchup crisps
    sandwiched together
    a veritable vinegar delight
    coffeecrisps & wunderbars
    you taught me
    the art of dim sum
    sticky rice & boiled pork bao
    garlic & hoisin blanched greens
    balanced betwixt my determined
    yet questionably sloppy
    sticks
    how is it
    no matter where we find
    ourselves
    you are
    my home
    sanctuary

326 tiny white forms
    unmoving
    impenetrable
    room enough
    for a fledgling calf
    no more
    no crime committed
    no trial or verdict
    only a life sentence
    solitary confinement
    no chance of contact
    with the world
    no opportunity
    to explore
    grow
    nuzzle
    frolic
    tears form
    at the corner of my eyes
    my heart aches
    at the inhumanity
    we're capable of
    the senseless
    torture

327 frothy green tea
    whisked with milk
    laden with marbles
    obsidian tapioca pearls
    a strong flavor
    of freshly
    pulverized
    grass

328 pre twitter status updates
    posted with care
    on now defunct currencies
    quick & dirty insights
    into the life
    of a stranger
    penned in abbreviations
    a language unknown
    few words still legible
    after having made its journey
    across state lines
    oceans
    decades
    lifetimes

                    329 this morning finds me
                        foraging
                        through an age worn
                        weather beaten
                        cardboard box
                        its contents somehow
                        protected
                        from the years of neglect
                        thousands of postcards
                        snippets of stories
                        chronicles of adventures
                        experiences had
                        by strangers
                        i'll never know

330 his name is
     tree
     the man sharing
     the bar
     his stories
     adventures
     life lessons
     dreams
     regrets
     with me

                    33I he tell me
                        of the experiences
                        that have molded
                        his life
                        his music
                        following the sound
                        the spirit
                        as it's lead him
                        from the pnw
                        his roots
                        to god's country
                        where the wind
                        began
                        the flatlands
                        the southern coast
                        willie & the hoodoo blues
                        god
                        dr. john

332 it was a wednesday
    the world's fair
    in seattle
    was over
    elvis had gone
    home
    i was tired
    of painting
    my mother's eaves
    in the blistering
    summer heat
    so i joined the army
    i left that friday
    to paint eaves
    for the government
    been on my own
    ever since

    life lessons gleaned
    from the memories
    of a 72 year old vet
    in the eastern washington
    summer sun

333 she stumbles
    her legs
    unsteady
    carrying her
    with great
    difficulty
    effort
    along the cracked
    crumbling
    sidewalk
    her attention
    devoted
    to the wheelchair
    she pushes
    and the puppy
    settled inside

334 how could he
    have rejected
    me
    i'm beautiful
    intelligent
    witty
    kind
    she mutters
    for the seventh
    time
    into the safe space
    hidden away
    at the bottom
    of her glass

335 sterling grey
    frocked
    fancy city chickens
    fluttering
    flitting
    from rooftop
    to balcony
    ledge

336 she always preferred
    pencils to pens
    lead to ink
    fragility
    finesse
    the ability
    to erase
    restart
    shade
    perfect

POST CARD.

THE ADDRESS ONLY TO BE WRITTEN HERE.

337 your supposed innocence
    at being only a bystander
    not embroiled in the fray
    your hands clear
    of blood
    your conscience free
    of guilt
    is a lie
    a line you repeat
    to yourself
    loud enough
    for others to hear
    your never ending
    tireless attempt
    to convince yourself
    of its truth

338 i've always preferred
    pens
    ink
    permanence
    stability
    unwavering statements
    unapologetic
    about flights
    of fancy
    changes
    in direction or truth

339 she's dripping in jewelry
costume pieces of jade
plastic beads
painted silver
chipping as they click
clack
against each other
with every exaggerated move
she carries a fan
wears electric yellow
fishnet
fingerless gloves

340 daddy long legs
spindly & fluid
a wisp more
than nothing
nearly invisible
without the perfect
hint
of light
teetering along
the sun pinked
underside
of an unsuspecting
thigh
weightlessly balanced
en pointe

341 we climb
    hillsides
    cresting
    within the
    clouds
    the moon
    full
    pressed against
    the summer
    sky
    shines down
    on eagle nests
    now level
    with our eyes

342 she reads him
    the menu
    to wear glasses
    would spoil
    the hard leather
    aesthetic
    he worked
    for decades
    to perfect
    she's younger
    bottle blonde
    ridden hard
    put away wet
    as my grandfather
    used to say
    they're weathered
    aged
    passing the early
    evening
    singing along
    off tune
    time

343 he talks
to himself
to the figures
standing
within arms
reach
but visible only
through his minds
eye
he chatters
without
pause
for breath
exhausting
himself
in hopes
of being
heard

344 the birch trees
have eyes
staring
never
blinking
lined
in charcoal
forest
watchmen

345 a girl should always have
a swivel chair
at the bar
to survey the place
her choices
options
prey
she tells me
reapplying another coat
of deep
oxygenated blood
red
lipstick

346 a slice
    of the berlin wall
    here
    in idaho
    worlds away
    pilfered
    treasured
    revered
    remembered

                        347 the bar
                            ordinarily a quiet
                            watering hole
                            for single gents
                            blue collar
                            working
                            folk
                            stopping only long enough
                            for a brew
                            tonight
                            filled to capacity
                            with octogenarians
                            on the prowl
                            veins pulsing
                            with vitamin v
                            fueled by
                            oyster shooters
                            little blue pills
                            poorly interpreted
                            oldies

348 they fall more
and more
in lust
with every
shaky
step
lured
onto the worn
dance floor
by the offbeat
irregular
rhythm
of tonight's
local
cover
band

349 the oversize
exaggerated
acrylic gems
sparkling
from the rear
pockets
of her overpriced
jeans
must leave
a bruise
if she ever
deigns
to plop

350 the thorn laden branches
climb
effortlessly scaling
dwarfing
the humble walls
windows
of my kitchen
not unlike
the bewitched
brambles
ensconcing
the fairy tale
resting place
of one
miss sleeping beauty

351 what if
    oxygen
    is the drug
    keeping us all
    from seeing
    the world
    as it really
    is

                    352 he broke down
                        deep
                        heaving
                        sobs
                        his eyes
                        pleading
                        for an answer
                        ripping
                        my heart
                        struggling
                        to be strong
                        to comfort
                        support
                        the strongest man
                        i've known
                        will know
                        brought
                        to his knees
                        by two syllables
                        one word
                        cancer

353 my grandfather was
born in panama
to a military family
of pnw natives
taught to smoke
drink
by my nanny
a suspender
aficionado
lover of bingo
cowboys & indians
before it was
a bad word
shooting marbles
until he matured
to guns

my grandfather was
a strong willed man
hardened
by the things he'd
seen
done
softened
by the adoration
of his
grandchildren

my grandfather was
proud
of his career
his medals
honors
accomplishments
his children
grandchildren
progeny
strong
broken only by news
of his soul mate
my nanny
passing away
his own
cancer diagnosis
mortality

my grandfather loved
steak
cooked rare
creamed spinach
white cake
with strawberries
ice cream
spooned straight
from the carton

354 i'd never seen him
    cry
    the doctor
    crouched
    his face
    inches away
    as if whispering
    the diagnosis
    sentence
    might soften
    the blow

355 a faded polaroid
    a moment
    frozen
    showing the childs
    sun kissed
    pinchable cheeks
    splashing
    giddy with
    excitement
    her first
    swimming pool
    a bucket
    split pea hued
    filled with
    love
    pot after pot
    of water
    warmed
    on the stove
    inside

356 a tin pan
    clenched firmly
    by her chubby
    toddler
    hands
    pilfered from
    the kitchen
    no longer
    a tool
    but
    an instrument

357 i remember
cold winter mornings
so dark
you couldn't tell
without checking
the clock
if it was day
or night
waking up
before anyone else
our house still
quiet
sound
asleep

i remember moving
softly
slowly
from the lower bunk
to the doorway
my arms
laden
with the weight
of my pillow
books
smaller than they are
today
already
strong
enough

i remember
making my way
to the back
of the house
taking care
stepping over
loose boards
warped by time
spots
that would tattle
give away
my presence
escape

i remember
our living room
cluttered
with objects
mementos
proof
of lives
being lived
love
being shared

i remember
tiptoeing
across
the cool laminate
of our humble kitchen
the heart
of our home
its pattern etched
into my memories
braille-like
in the dark
against the soles
of my naked feet

i remember
slipping unnoticed
into the solace
of our small
shared bathroom
a tiny nightlight
a single
flickering star
within the dark

i remember
the floor
a thick blue carpet
once deep enough
to burrow toes
long before
i was ever
imagined

i remember
the silent darkness
our bathroom
at midnight
it was my sanctuary
hideaway
a place
i could escape
the world
my family
serious issues
gnawing at
my young
impressionable
spirit

i remember
sitting
in the corner
as close as i dared
to the small
space heater
my shins tingling
hot to the touch
while i lost
myself
in the pages of a book
a world
different
far away
from my own

358 he chuckles
    as he tells me
    the story
    of septic dave
    a local
    stubborn
    crass
    ass
    no longer
    full of piss
    vinegar
    after finding
    himself
    6 shots deep
    at the wrong end
    of a large
    barreled
    handgun

359 his blue eyes
    sparkle
    pnw tide pools
    sliced with shards
    of glass
    ice
    they squint
    glisten
    smile
    with fond memories
    remembered
    relived

360 lumber
    flammable bodies
    slaughtered
    straightened
    stacked
    forming a mosaic
    of wood grain
    echoing rings
    marking decades
    of life
    experience
    time

361 the shower & car
are my safe
places
where i feel
i can break
down
allowing my guard
to fall
with the tears
i hold
so tightly
to my chest

362 nowstalgia
the feeling
of longing
to replicate
the now
aching
to prolong
the present

363 his name is joe
his smile
is contagious
as he beckons me
through his
labyrinth
of beasts
birthed
from his
imagination
their driftwood
bones
scattering
the lawn
pilfered
foraged
found

364 i peek
every morning
watching
as the colors
shift
bright tadpole green
to deep
onyx obsidian
the flesh plumping
nearly bursting
at the softest
nudge
of a chickadees
beak
as they race me
to harvest
your nectar

365 a bear
relaxed
belly dusting
the double yellow
lines
of the dark
moon lit highway
we laugh
to break the tension
of the near life
ending
mortality testing
moment
we liken him
to an overgrown
prepubescent boy
having experimented
with pot
enjoying a late night
case
of the munchies

This Space for Writing Messages

POST CARD

Place
Stamp Here
Domestic
One cent
Foreign
Two cents

For address only

about the author

Megs is a professional word-twerker, book-doula, intuitive writing coach, ghostwriter, author & publisher based in the heart of Montana.

After spending 20+ years trying to fit into someone else's box in the corporate world, afraid of what might happen if she swam against the current, Megs decided to leave her health insurance, paid vacation & regular paychecks behind to start her own business, following her passion & purpose.

When she's not playing with words, Megs can be found exploring rabbit holes & fueling her slight obsession with all things true crime, coffee, cryptids, and cults, or working on her latest quilting project.

For more info about Megs visit her websites, www.megswrites.com & www.inomniaparatuspublishing.com, connect with her via FB (@megsthompson), IG (@megs.writes), send her an email (megs@megswrites.com), or join out her virtual writing group, just write: accountability & educational community for writers.

www.ingramcontent.com/pod-product-compliance
Lightning Source LLC
Chambersburg PA
CBHW071151120626
46546CB00006B/2216